The Art of Drowning

The Art of Drowning

Billy Collins

University of Pittsburgh Press
Pittsburgh • London

The publication of this book is supported by a grant from the Pennsylvania Council on the Arts.

Published by the University of Pittsburgh Press, Pittsburgh, Pa. 15260
Copyright © 1995, Billy Collins
All rights reserved
Manufactured in the United States of America
Printed on acid-free paper

20 19 18 17 16 15 14 13 12 11

Library of Congress Cataloging-in-Publication Data

Collins, Billy.
  The art of drowning / Billy Collins.
      p.   cm. —(Pitt poetry series)
  ISBN 0-8229-3893-6 (alk. paper).—ISBN 0-8229-5567-9 (pbk.: alk. paper)
  I. Title.   II. Series.
  PS3553.047478A84 1995   95-3297
  811'.54—dc20   CIP

The author and publisher wish to express their grateful acknowledgment to the following publications in which these poems (some in earlier versions) first appeared: *The American Poetry Review* ("Shoveling Snow with Buddha," "Some Final Words," "Sweet Talk"); *The American Scholar* ("Monday Morning"); *Boulevard* ("The City of Tomorrow"); *Chelsea* ("Shadow"); *Chicago Review* ("Reading in a Hammock"); *Crazyhorse* ("Dream," "Nightclub"); *Folio* ("Driving Myself to a Poetry Reading"); *The Journal* ("The Blues," "Exploring the Coast of Birdland"); *OntheBus* ("Piano Lessons"); *The Paris Review* ("My Heart," "On Turning Ten," "Sunday Morning With the Sensational Nightingales," "Workshop"); *The Plum Review* ("Man in Space"); *Poetry* ("The Art of Drowning," "The Best Cigarette," "The Biography of a Cloud," "Cheers," "Dancing Toward Bethlehem," "Days," "Dear Reader," "The End of the World," "Fiftieth Birthday Eve," "Influence," "Medium," "Osso Buco," "Pinup," "Romanticism," "Thesaurus," "Tuesday, June 4, 1991," "While Eating a Pear"); *TriQuarterly* ("Design," "Directions"); *West Branch* ("Budapest," "Horizon"); and *Wordsmith* ("Conversion," "Print").

"Tuesday, June 4, 1991" also appeared in *The Best American Poetry 1993* edited by Louis Glück and David Lehman.

"Canada" first appeared in *The Gettysburg Review,* Volume 8, Number 2, and is reprinted here by permission of the editors.

"Metropolis" originally appeared in *The New Yorker.*

The author wishes to thank the John Simon Guggenheim Foundation for a fellowship which supported the writing of many of these poems. Thanks also to Dan Brown for his sharp editorial eye, to Chris Calhoun for his buoyant encouragement, and to Diane, for everything.

Painting: J.M.W. Turner, *Dawn After the Wreck,* courtesy of Courtauld Institue Galleries, London.

Author photo: Joanne Carney
Book Design: Frank Lehner

For Tom Wallace (1942–1993)

Where did that dog
that used to be here go?
I thought about him
once again tonight
before I went to bed.

—SHIMAKI AKAHIKO

Contents

IV

The Art of Drowning

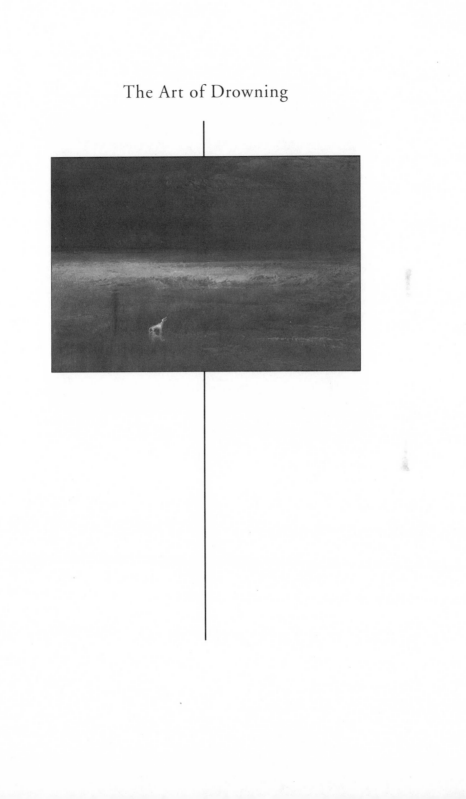

Dear Reader

Baudelaire considers you his brother,
and Fielding calls out to you every few paragraphs
as if to make sure you have not closed the book,
and now I am summoning you up again,
attentive ghost, dark silent figure standing
in the doorway of these words.

Pope welcomes you into the glow of his study,
takes down a leather-bound Ovid to show you.
Tennyson lifts the latch to a moated garden,
and with Yeats you lean against a broken pear tree,
the day hooded by low clouds.

But now you are here with me,
composed in the open field of this page,
no room or manicured garden to enclose us,
no Zeitgeist marching in the background,
no heavy ethos thrown over us like a cloak.

Instead, our meeting is so brief and accidental,
unnoticed by the monocled eye of History,
you could be the man I held the door for
this morning at the bank or post office
or the one who wrapped my speckled fish.
You could be someone I passed on the street
or the face behind the wheel of an oncoming car.

The sunlight flashes off your windshield,
and when I look up into the small, posted mirror,
I watch you diminish—my echo, my twin—
and vanish around a curve in this whip
of a road we can't help traveling together.

I

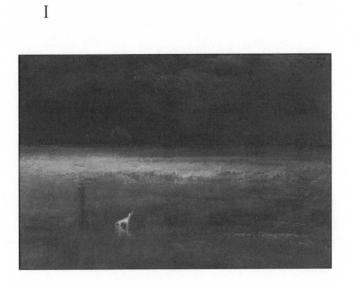

Consolation

How agreeable it is not to be touring Italy this summer,
wandering her cities and ascending her torrid hilltowns.
How much better to cruise these local, familiar streets,
fully grasping the meaning of every roadsign and billboard
and all the sudden hand gestures of my compatriots.

There are no abbeys here, no crumbling frescoes or famous
domes and there is no need to memorize a succession
of kings or tour the dripping corners of a dungeon.
No need to stand around a sarcophagus, see Napoleon's
little bed on Elba, or view the bones of a saint under glass.

How much better to command the simple precinct of home
than be dwarfed by pillar, arch, and basilica.
Why hide my head in phrase books and wrinkled maps?
Why feed scenery into a hungry, one-eyed camera
eager to eat the world one monument at a time?

Instead of slouching in a café ignorant of the word for ice,
I will head down to the coffee shop and the waitress
known as Dot. I will slide into the flow of the morning
paper, all language barriers down,
rivers of idiom running freely, eggs over easy on the way.

And after breakfast, I will not have to find someone
willing to photograph me with my arm around the owner.
I will not puzzle over the bill or record in a journal
what I had to eat and how the sun came in the window.
It is enough to climb back into the car

as if it were the great car of English itself
and sounding my loud vernacular horn, speed off
down a road that will never lead to Rome, not even Bologna.

Osso Buco

I love the sound of the bone against the plate
and the fortress-like look of it
lying before me in a moat of risotto,
the meat soft as the leg of an angel
who has lived a purely airborne existence.
And best of all, the secret marrow,
the invaded privacy of the animal
prized out with a knife and swallowed down
with cold, exhilarating wine.

I am swaying now in the hour after dinner,
a citizen tilted back on his chair,
a creature with a full stomach—
something you don't hear much about in poetry,
that sanctuary of hunger and deprivation.
You know: the driving rain, the boots by the door,
small birds searching for berries in winter.

But tonight, the lion of contentment
has placed a warm, heavy paw on my chest,
and I can only close my eyes and listen
to the drums of woe throbbing in the distance
and the sound of my wife's laughter
on the telephone in the next room,
the woman who cooked the savory osso buco,
who pointed to show the butcher the ones she wanted.
She who talks to her faraway friend
while I linger here at the table
with a hot, companionable cup of tea,
feeling like one of the friendly natives,
a reliable guide, maybe even the chief's favorite son.

Somewhere, a man is crawling up a rocky hillside
on bleeding knees and palms, an Irish penitent
carrying the stone of the world in his stomach;
and elsewhere people of all nations stare
at one another across a long, empty table.

But here, the candles give off their warm glow,
the same light that Shakespeare and Izaac Walton wrote by,
the light that lit and shadowed the faces of history.
Only now it plays on the blue plates,
the crumpled napkins, the crossed knife and fork.

In a while, one of us will go up to bed
and the other one will follow.
Then we will slip below the surface of the night
into miles of water, drifting down and down
to the dark, soundless bottom
until the weight of dreams pulls us lower still,
below the shale and layered rock,
beneath the strata of hunger and pleasure,
into the broken bones of the earth itself,
into the marrow of the only place we know.

Directions

You know the brick path in back of the house,
the one you see from the kitchen window,
the one that bends around the far end of the garden
where all the yellow primroses are?
And you know how if you leave the path
and walk up into the woods you come
to a heap of rocks, probably pushed
down during the horrors of the Ice Age,
and a grove of tall hemlocks, dark green now
against the light brown fallen leaves?
And farther on, you know
the small footbridge with the broken railing
and if you go beyond that you arrive
at the bottom of that sheep's head hill?
Well, if you start climbing, and you
might have to grab hold of a sapling
when the going gets steep,
you will eventually come to a long stone
ridge with a border of pine trees
which is as high as you can go
and a good enough place to stop.

The best time is late afternoon
when the sun strobes through
the columns of trees as you are hiking up,
and when you find an agreeable rock
to sit on, you will be able to see
the light pouring down into the woods
and breaking into the shapes and tones
of things and you will hear nothing

but a sprig of birdsong or the leafy
falling of a cone or nut through the trees,
and if this is your day you might even
spot a hare or feel the wing-beats of geese
driving overhead toward some destination.

But it is hard to speak of these things
how the voices of light enter the body
and begin to recite their stories
how the earth holds us painfully against
its breast made of humus and brambles
how we who will soon be gone regard
the entities that continue to return
greener than ever, spring water flowing
through a meadow and the shadows of clouds
passing over the hills and the ground
where we stand in the tremble of thought
taking the vast outside into ourselves.

Still, let me know before you set out.
Come knock on my door
and I will walk with you as far as the garden
with one hand on your shoulder.
I will even watch after you and not turn back
to the house until you disappear
into the crowd of maple and ash,
heading up toward the hill,
piercing the ground with your stick.

Influence

All these years and I never realized
why I found the mourning dove so interesting
until you pointed out
that morning we stood by the icy window
its resemblance to Robert Penn Warren—
the secretive eyes, soft royal neck,
and the mild, unruffled demeanor.

It was the day after a garrulous night
of champagne and shrimp, lamb and red wine,
and we were watching a huddle of them
pecking around in the fresh snow under the feeder
(Pulitzer Prize winners all),
and your comment, so astute and perfectly weird,
made me feel enclosed again in the coded talk
of friendship, that tall pagoda
where companions can sit on pillows
and observe the great China of life filing by
and say whatever comes to mind.

Steam curlicued up from the tea,
a recorded horn was noodling in the background,
and I forget what else was said
unless it was that the long necks of aristocrats
accounted for the popularity of the guillotine.
Then we all said good-bye and you and Louise
waved your way down the driveway
and drove off in the clear winter light.

But for days afterward, whenever I saw the doves
milling around in the snow,
their legs thin as pencil leads,

I found myself thinking of *All the King's Men,*
picturing the cover of the paperback
I used to carry around in my jacket pocket.

I even began to wonder, as the sun nudged
the shadows of the bare trees across the snow,
whether the titmouse, fluttering about
in its own tiny sphere of excitement,
did not remind me somewhat of Marianne Moore.

Water Table

It is on dry sunny days like this one that I find myself
thinking about the enormous body of water
that lies under this house,
cool, unseen reservoir,
silent except for the sounds of dripping
and the incalculable shifting
of all the heavy darkness that it holds.

This is the water that our well was dug to sip
and lift to where we live,
water drawn up and falling on our bare shoulders,
water filling the inlets of our mouths,
water in a pot on the stove.

The house is nothing now but a blueprint of pipes,
a network of faucets, nozzles, and spigots,
and even outdoors where light pierces the air
and clouds fly over the canopies of trees,
my thoughts flow underground
trying to imagine the cavernous scene.

Surely it is no pool with a colored ball
floating on the blue surface.
No grotto where a king would have
his guests rowed around in swan-shaped boats.
Between the dark lakes where the dark rivers flow
there is no ferry waiting on the shore of rock
and no man holding a long oar,
ready to take your last coin.
This is the real earth and the real water it contains.

But some nights, I must tell you,
I go down there after everyone has fallen asleep.
I swim back and forth in the echoing blackness.
I sing a love song as well as I can,
lost for a while in the home of the rain.

Reading in a Hammock

With one arm raised, I am holding
The Penguin Book of French Verse over my head,
assuming one of the standard positions of summer,
looking up into this little sky of words.

Around the edges of the book is the larger sky,
dotted with clouds, and some overhanging branches
that appear to be slowly swaying back and forth,
as if I were the one lying motionless,

calmly thumbing through Verlaine and Baudelaire
while the world around me slides from side to side
in the lazy rhythm of a hammock.
Whatever is doing the actual swinging would matter

little to Apollinaire who thought religion
looked like a hangar on an airfield and
whose angels plucked geese and wore chef's hats,
and the drowsier I become the less it matters to me.

Finally rocked beyond words, I close the book
on all the drolleries and the anguishing,
all the poems that have moved in my hands
like butterflies among the flowers of evil.

Above, a soft light shines through an opening
in the two dark maples that are the poles of my dangling.
A light so pale and violet it is impossible
to tell if I am a man of leisure

or a martyr to idleness, tied to these trees,
condemned to swing gently in the shade until dead.

Print

In the dining room there is a brown fish
hanging on the wall who swims along
in his frame while we are eating dinner.

He swims in candlelight for all to see,
as if he has been swimming forever, even
in the darkness of the ink before someone thought

to draw him and the thin reeds waving in his stream
and the clear pebbles strewn upon the sand.
No wonder he continues his swimming

deep into the night, long after we have
blown out the candles and gone upstairs to bed.
No wonder I find him in the pale morning

light, still swimming, still looking out at me
with his one, small, spellbound eye.

Sunday Morning with the Sensational Nightingales

It was not the Five Mississippi Blind Boys
who lifted me off the ground
that Sunday morning
as I drove down for the paper, some oranges, and bread.
Nor was it the Dixie Hummingbirds
or the Soul Stirrers, despite their quickening name,
or even the Swan Silvertones
who inspired me to look over the commotion of trees
into the open vault of the sky.

No, it was the Sensational Nightingales
who happened to be singing on the gospel
station early that Sunday morning
and must be credited with the bumping up
of my spirit, the arousal of the mice within.

I have always loved this harmony,
like four, sometimes five trains running
side by side over a contoured landscape—
make that a shimmering, red-dirt landscape,
wildflowers growing along the silver tracks,
lace tablecloths covering the hills,
the men and women in white shirts and dresses
walking in the direction of a tall steeple.
Sunday morning in a perfect Georgia.

But I am not here to describe the sound
of the falsetto whine, sepulchral bass,
alto and tenor fitted snugly in between;
only to witness my own minor ascension

that morning as they sang, so parallel,
about the usual themes,
the garden of suffering,
the beads of blood on the forehead,
the stone before the hillside tomb,
and the ancient rolling waters
we would all have to cross some day.

God bless the Sensational Nightingales,
I thought as I turned up the volume,
God bless their families and their powder blue suits.
They are a far cry from the quiet kneeling
I was raised with,
a far, hand-clapping cry from the candles
that glowed in the alcoves
and the fixed eyes of saints staring down
from their corners.

Oh, my cap was on straight that Sunday morning
and I was fine keeping the car on the road.
No one would ever have guessed
I was being lifted into the air by nightingales,
hoisted by their beaks like a long banner
that curls across an empty blue sky,
caught up in the annunciation
of these high, most encouraging tidings.

Cheers

Already tonight I have lifted my glass to Jackie
Wilson and to Gracie Lantz, the voice
of Woody Woodpecker and creator of the taunting laugh
according to her obituary in this morning's paper.

And now the wind is whistling at the doors and windows,
straining to lift the roof off this house,
and I am alone and casting about for someone else
to toast, someone remarkable whose leaving

shrivels the skin of the world. It could be
a virgin martyr or exiled Ovid, or even Jackie
Wilson again, the man no act would follow,
not James Brown, not the Temptations, one of whom

explained it was because he left a hole in the stage.
The only toast that should follow a toast to the dead
is a toast to the long dead, so up goes my glass
to the first man ever to notice the outline

of a bear in the stars one quiet night long before
the wheel and shortly after fire. It is said
that laziness was the mother of astronomy,
and surely he must have spent hours on his back,

hands pillowing his head, while his eyes
connected the points of light with imaginary lines
until a ferocious shape stood before him in the sky.
I drink to the long wonderment of his gazing,

the Nile of amazement flowing into the night,
his hand moving up to cover his open mouth.

And still the wind is driving hard through the trees,
knocking down the weak branches which I will

gather in the morning and break over my knee
for kindling; but the scene inside is composed,
a tableau of bottle, vase, open book,
a painting of a little ship framed on the wall,

far from home in a churning sea and burdened
with perilous cargo. I wander in the details
of its sail lines and streamers flying from the masts.
I see a man in the rigging, the red dot of his shirt.

No wonder visitors always remark on this picture
while I am out in the kitchen making their drinks
and getting ready to propose the first toast,
to hoist my glass to that dark, bearded man

lying dumbstruck and reeking of woodsmoke
a little distance from the mouth of his cave.
Here's to the bear he saw roaring in the heavens,
to the ram, the tilted scales, the intricate crab,

and the dippers pouring out a universe of ink.
Here's to Cassiopeia in her chair and chained Andromeda.
Here's to the wind blowing against this lighted house
and to the vast, windless spaces between the stars.

The Best Cigarette

There are many that I miss,
having sent my last one out a car window
sparking along the road one night, years ago.

The heralded ones, of course:
after sex, the two glowing tips
now the lights of a single ship;
at the end of a long dinner
with more wine to come
and a smoke ring coasting into the chandelier;
or on a white beach,
holding one with fingers still wet from a swim.

How bittersweet these punctuations
of flame and gesture;
but the best were on those mornings
when I would have a little something going
in the typewriter,
the sun bright in the windows,
maybe some Berlioz on in the background.
I would go into the kitchen for coffee
and on the way back to the page,
curled in its roller,
I would light one up and feel
its dry rush mix with the dark taste of coffee.

Then I would be my own locomotive,
trailing behind me as I returned to work
little puffs of smoke,
indicators of progress,
signs of industry and thought,
the signal that told the nineteenth century

it was moving forward.
That was the best cigarette,
when I would steam into the study
full of vaporous hope
and stand there,
the big headlamp of my face
pointed down at all the words in parallel lines.

Metropolis

These are my favorite museum rooms,
the out-of-the-way ones on the upper floors,
usually unpeopled except for a single guard
who appears and disappears in the maze of walls
where these minor American paintings are hung.

I like the calm rustic ones: a surface of lake,
the low bough of an oak like a long arm,
a blue smudge of distant hills,
anything with cows, especially if they are standing
in a stream, their large, vacuous faces
staring into the warm, nineteenth-century afternoon.
And if one has lowered her head to drink
and the painter has indicated with flecks of white
the water pouring down from the animal's mouth,
then the day, I feel, has achieved a modest crest.

And if it is raining outside that day
and low clouds press down on city buildings
while people under umbrellas climb the marble steps,
I usually find myself in front of the still lifes,
those painstaking devotions to objects,
agreeable possessions laid out on the altar of a table.

I will examine the rim of a crystal pitcher,
the glint of candlelight on a silver spoon,
a curve of violin, the russet feathers of a grouse.
I will put on my glasses and study
this group of pears, this curling page of music,
this flute, inkwell, or dinner bell,
these wooden matches beautifully strewn
upon the dark green velvet cloth.

This is when I feel the tongs of the world
letting go of me, so I can float suspended
in the air around these glistening things
whose shadows will never lengthen
and whose weight no hand will ever feel.

You can have that bronze sculpture by the elevators:
"Revolution Holding the Head of Error
and Standing Over the Cadaver of Monarchy."
My place is here, leaning forward, wandering
through the microscopic, eyelash details of
"Still Life with Herring, Wine, and Cheese,"
"Still Life with Tobacco, Grapes, and a Pocket Watch,"
"Still Life with Porcelain Vase, Silver Tray, and Glasses,"

or the one that always sends me out the door,
returns me, humming like a gyroscope,
to the rain and the madhouse outcries of the streets:
"Still Life with Wild Strawberries in a Wan Li Bowl."

Days

Each one *is* a gift, no doubt,
mysteriously placed in your waking hand
or set upon your forehead
moments before you open your eyes.

Today begins cold and bright,
the ground heavy with snow
and the thick masonry of ice,
the sun glinting off the turrets of clouds.

Through the calm eye of the window
everything is in its place
but so precariously
this day might be resting somehow

on the one before it,
all the days of the past stacked high
like the impossible tower of dishes
entertainers used to build on stage.

No wonder you find yourself
perched on the top of a tall ladder
hoping to add one more.
Just another Wednesday

you whisper,
then holding your breath,
place this cup on yesterday's saucer
without the slightest clink.

Tuesday, June 4, 1991

By the time I get myself out of bed, my wife has left
the house to take her botany final and the painter
has arrived in his van and is already painting
the columns of the front porch white and the decking gray.

It is early June, a breezy and sun-riddled Tuesday
that would quickly be forgotten were it not for my
writing these few things down as I sit here empty-headed
at the typewriter with a cup of coffee, light and sweet.

I feel like the secretary to the morning whose only
responsibility is to take down its bright, airy dictation
until it's time to go to lunch with the other girls,
all of us ordering the cottage cheese with half a pear.

This is what stenographers do in courtrooms, too,
alert at their miniature machines taking down every word.
When there is a silence they sit still as I do, waiting
and listening, fingers resting lightly on the keys.

This is also what Samuel Pepys did, jotting down in
private ciphers minor events that would have otherwise
slipped into the dark amnesiac waters of the Thames.
His vigilance finally paid off when London caught fire

as mine does when the painter comes in for coffee
and says how much he likes this slow vocal rendition
of "You Don't Know What Love Is" and I figure I will
make him a tape when he goes back to his brushes and pails.

Under the music I can hear the rush of cars and trucks
on the highway and every so often the new kitten, Felix,

hops into my lap and watches my fingers drumming out
a running record of this particular June Tuesday

as it unrolls before my eyes, a long intricate carpet
that I am walking on slowly with my head bowed
knowing that it is leading me to the quiet shrine
of the afternoon and the melancholy candles of evening.

If I look up, I see out the window the white stars
of clematis climbing a ladder of strings, a woodpile,
a stack of faded bricks, a small green garden of herbs,
things you would expect to find outside a window,

all written down now and placed in the setting
of a stanza as unalterably as they are seated
in their chairs in the ontological rooms of the world.
Yes, this is the kind of job I could succeed in,

an unpaid but contented amanuensis whose hands
are two birds fluttering on the lettered keys,
whose eyes see sunlight splashing through the leaves,
and the bright pink asterisks of honeysuckle

and the piano at the other end of this room with
its small vase of faded flowers and its empty bench.
So convinced am I that I have found my vocation,
tomorrow I will begin my chronicling earlier, at dawn,

a time when hangmen and farmers are up and doing,
when men holding pistols stand in a field back to back.
It is the time the ancients imagined in robes, as Eos
or Aurora, who would leave her sleeping husband in bed,

not to take her botany final, but to pull the sun,
her brother, over the horizon's brilliant rim,
her four-horse chariot aimed at the zenith of the sky.
But tomorrow, dawn will come the way I picture her,

barefoot and disheveled, standing outside my window
in one of the fragile cotton dresses of the poor.
She will look in at me with her thin arms extended,
offering a handful of birdsong and a small cup of light.

II

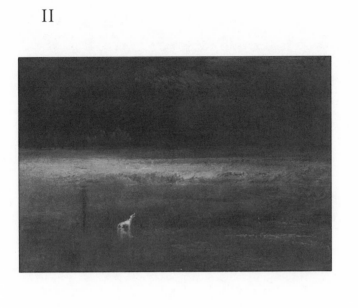

The Art of Drowning

I wonder how it all got started, this business
about seeing your life flash before your eyes
while you drown, as if panic, or the act of submergence,
could startle time into such compression, crushing
decades in the vice of your desperate, final seconds.

After falling off a steamship or being swept away
in a rush of floodwaters, wouldn't you hope
for a more leisurely review, an invisible hand
turning the pages of an album of photographs—
you up on a pony or blowing out candles in a conic hat.

How about a short animated film, a slide presentation?
Your life expressed in an essay, or in one model paragraph?
Wouldn't any form be better than this sudden flash?
Your whole existence going off in your face
in an eyebrow-singeing explosion of biography—
nothing like the three large volumes you envisioned.

Survivors would have us believe in a brilliance
here, some bolt of truth forking across the water,
an ultimate Light before all the lights go out,
dawning on you with all its megalithic tonnage.
But if something does flash before your eyes
as you go under, it will probably be a fish,

a quick blur of curved silver darting away,
having nothing to do with your life or your death.
The tide will take you, or the lake will accept it all
as you sink toward the weedy disarray of the bottom,
leaving behind what you have already forgotten,
the surface, now overrun with the high travel of clouds.

Canada

I am writing this on a strip of white birch bark
that I cut from a tree with a pen knife.
There is no other way to express adequately
the immensity of the clouds that are passing over the farms
and wooded lakes of Ontario and the endless visibility
that hands you the horizon on a platter.

I am also writing this in a wooden canoe,
a point of balance in the middle of Lake Couchiching,
resting the birch bark against my knees.
I can feel the sun's hands on my bare back,
but I am thinking of winter,
snow piled up in all the provinces
and the solemnity of the long grain ships
that pass the cold months moored at Owen Sound.

O Canada, as the anthem goes,
scene of my boyhood summers,
you are the pack of Sweet Caporals on the table,
you are the dove-soft train whistle in the night,
you are the empty chair at the end of an empty dock.
You are the shelves of books in a lakeside cottage:
Gift from the Sea by Anne Morrow Lindbergh,
A Child's Garden of Verses by Robert Louis Stevenson,
Anne of Avonlea by L. M. Montgomery,
So You're Going to Paris! by Clara E. Laughlin,
and *Peril Over the Airport,* one
of the Vicky Barr Flight Stewardess series
by Helen Wills whom some will remember
as the author of the Cherry Ames Nurse stories.

What has become of the languorous girls
who would pass the long limp summer evenings reading
Cherry Ames, Student Nurse, Cherry Ames, Senior Nurse,
Cherry Ames, Chief Nurse, and *Cherry Ames, Flight Nurse?*
Where are they now, the ones who shared her adventures
as a veterans' nurse, private duty nurse, visiting nurse,
cruise nurse, night supervisor, mountaineer nurse,
dude ranch nurse (there is little she has not done),
rest home nurse, department store nurse,
boarding school nurse, and country doctor's nurse?

O Canada, I have not forgotten you,
and as I kneel in my canoe, beholding this vision
of a bookcase, I pray that I remain in your vast,
polar, North American memory.
You are the paddle, the snowshoe, the cabin in the pines.
You are Jean de Brébeuf with his martyr's necklace of hatchet heads.
You are the moose in the clearing and the moosehead on the wall.
You are the rapids, the propeller, the kerosene lamp.
You are the dust that coats the roadside berries.
But not only that.
You are the two boys with pails walking along that road,
and one of them, the taller one minus the straw hat, is me.

The Biography of a Cloud

It would have been easier to follow Johnson
from pub to pub with a notebook and pen
or sift through cardboard boxes
crammed with Trollopiana
than to tell the story of this anonymous mass.

It is hard to say even where it was born,
though considering its thick, whipped texture
and its lofty, processional manner,
I have it somewhere over a large warm body of water,
fathered by heat, mothered by humidity.

We do know this much:
that it billowed white at the mountainous top
and its flat underside was the gray of headstones;
that it slid onto the land and felt its way
over the contours of several western states,
always moving eastward, from left to right
the way the eyes move over print
as if it were reading the earth with its blind shadow.

Otherwise, it did nothing
but allow itself to be blown through the high cold atmosphere,
though it was always changing shape,
and assumed in its lifetime the form
of Australia, the head of an enormous dog,
a sheep on the run, a hippo with its mouth agape,
and even the camel that passed through the eye of Hamlet.

As usual, its existence was noted by only a few:
a workman eating lunch on a girder,
a woman on a terrace watering plants,

and a large number of people named Riley,
all supine in hammocks or on blankets spread for picnics.

Ordinarily it traveled in a convoy
or pedaled along with one or two companions,
but early one morning over Arizona
it held the distinction of being the only one in the sky.

In the end, it died as all clouds do,
in an obscurity befitting one of the minor English poets,
the son of a London hatter or an Essex clergyman,
sent down from Oxford for heresy or gambling,
soon addicted to laudanum, then the slide into destitution,
for their stories, too, begin to sound alike.

But I would rather track the life of a cloud
than labor over packets of letters
written in a crabbed hand
or explicate the four sorry volumes of verse
he would have left when he died,
gout-ridden on a cot in Wembley.

I prefer a wayside bench, ensnared by vines,
to the dark aisles of a library,
a place to watch them inch across the sky,
caravans plying their ancient trade routes.
I want to train my scholar's eye
on the bright shifting edges
where the weightless tongues of clouds lick the air.
I want to remove my hat, close my eyes,
and feel the sun, warm and intermittent, on my face.

Death Beds

The ancients were talkative on theirs,
so many agencies needed to be addressed:
the gods of departure who controlled
the seven portals of the world,
the ferrymen leaning on their smooth oars,
the eternal pilots, immortal conductors,
and that was just the transportation.

Japanese monks would motion for a tablet,
sometimes, an inkwell and a brush
so they could leave behind the dark,
wet strokes of a short poem—
a drop of rain on a yellow leaf.
One described the night clouds
and the moon making its million-mile journey.

Medieval Christians who could read
could read a treatise on the subject:
De Arte Moriendi, On the Art of Dying,
pages of instruction on what to do in bed,
how to set the heart right
how to point the soul upward
and listen to the prayer of one's own breathing.

Some pale Victorians in their tubercular
throes would ask for a looking glass
so they could behold the seraphic glow
the dry fever brought to their faces.
A few even had a photographer summoned
to open his tripod in the sickroom
and disappear under the heavy black cloth
as the subject, more or less, was doing the same.

Then there were the wits,
using their last breath to exhale a line,
a devastating capper, as if the world
were simply a large gallery buzzing with people,
and now it was time to throw on a long scarf
and make an exit, leaving
it to someone else to close the door.

Some lie on their backs for months,
students of the ceiling,
others roll over once and are gone.
Some bellow for a priest
and make the one confession no one doubts.
And you, and I, too, may lie on ours,
the vigilant family in a semicircle,
or the night nurse holding our hand
in the dark, or alone.
There will be no ink, mirror, or Latin book,
though the wallpaper may be tasteless
and you may feel yourself entering a myth.

I would hope for a window,
the usual frame of reference,
a clear sky, or thin high clouds,
an abundance of sun, a cool pillow.
And I would expect just at the end
a moment of pure awareness
when I could feel the solitary pea under the mattress
and pick out the dot of a hawk lost in the blue.

Conversion

I would like to spend the day on the slope
of a mountain, listening to a parable
about a lost sheep or a blighted vineyard.

For months my only companion would be this story,
and the more I told it to myself
the clearer everything would become.

Then, I would remove my helmet of opinions
and walk into the public streets
revealing the soft brown mushroom of my new head.

I would repeat the story to small groups of men
drawing illustrations in the sand with a stick.
I would leave them murmuring in a circle.

And late at night when the cold wind found
the chinks of my house
and disturbed the candle stub next to my bed,

I would hear the story told by the tongue of flame
and watch the shadows of my former self
flicker on the low ceiling and the walls of stone.

Horizon

You can use the brush of a Japanese monk
or a pencil stub from a race track.

As long as you draw the line a third
the way up from the bottom of the page,

the effect is the same: the world suddenly
divided into its elemental realms.

A moment ago there was only a piece of paper.
Now there is earth and sky, sky and sea.

You were sitting alone in a small room.
Now you are walking into the heat of a vast desert

or standing on the ledge of a winter beach
watching the light on the water, light in the air.

The City of Tomorrow

No matter which illustrator was called on
during the 1930s, '40s or '50s
to squint into the world of tomorrow
and render his impression,
the resulting drawing was always the same.
A city of tall, streamlined buildings,
bubble-shaped elevators running up the sides,
spiraling towers, vast oval terminals,
transparent pavilions, glassy arcades,
all connected by a complicated network
of ramps, monorails, and vaulted walkways,
and above it all, a sky busy with the traffic of strange craft:
jet dirigibles, flying omnibuses,
jumbo helicopters, and one-man winged torpedoes.
Even the air they flew in looked futuristic.

I would linger on these magazine pages
studying the brushed aluminum surface of things,
the little pen strokes indicating plate glass,
the perfectly artificial environment
completely enclosed in a huge dome
as if it were a city brought to your table,
a delicacy for the imagination to savor,
for this, I believed, was the city of my future.

I focused on the tiny human figures
waiting at a rooftop heliport or drifting along
an electronic sidewalk, heading for the office,
and I knew some day I would be one of them.
This city of clean lines was my inheritance,
and it would fall into my outstretched arms
as soon as the present grew old and died in its sleep.

But time never advanced, only turned
like the slow blades of the summer fan
over my bed where I would lie imagining
what it would be like to drive a plastic car,
speed lines coming off a giant fin,
to wear a chromium rocket on my back,
yes, wondering what it would be like
to recline high up in an apartment of the future,
pushing the buttons on a bedside console
while stroking the forehead of a beautiful robot.

I didn't know that the city of tomorrow
was not a place we would come to inhabit
but a place that inhabits us, a phantom
that draftsmen with rulers and India ink
would soon lose interest in drawing.

Never mind.
The city of the future I now envision
could be a city of ice, a city of candles,
a city of shoe horns or empty frames,
a city of desire and facing it,
across a river, a city of no desire.
It might not be a city at all, but a meadow of grass
where the horses of tomorrow will lower
their mild heads to graze,
or a vaporous landscape, the valleys flooded
with the dolorous chords of unwritten songs,
the mountain tops cold and forbidding,
waiting for the climbers of the future to seek them out.

Thesaurus

It could be the name of a prehistoric beast
that roamed the Paleozoic earth, rising up
on its hind legs to show off its large vocabulary,
or some lover in a myth who is metamorphosed into a book.

It means treasury, but it is just a place
where words congregate with their relatives,
a big park where hundreds of family reunions
are always being held,
house, home, abode, dwelling, lodgings, and *digs*
all sharing the same picnic basket and thermos;
hairy, hirsute, woolly, furry, fleecy, and *shaggy*
all running a sack race or throwing horseshoes,
inert, static, motionless, fixed and *immobile*
standing and kneeling in rows for a group photograph.

Here father is next to sire and brother close
to sibling, separated only by fine shades of meaning.
And every group has its odd cousin, the one
who traveled the farthest to be here:
astereognosis, polydipsia, or some eleven
syllable, unpronounceable substitute for the word *tool.*
Even their own relatives have to squint at their name tags.

I can see my own copy up on a high shelf.
I rarely open it, because I know there is no
such thing as a synonym and because I get nervous
around people who always assemble with their own kind,
forming clubs and nailing signs to closed front doors
while others huddle alone in the dark streets.

I would rather see words out on their own, away
from their families and the warehouse of Roget,
wandering the world where they sometimes fall
in love with a completely different word.
Surely, you have seen pairs of them standing forever
next to each other on the same line inside a poem,
a small chapel where weddings like these,
between perfect strangers, can take place.

Fiftieth Birthday Eve

The figure alone is enough to keep me wide awake,
the five with its little station master's belly
and cap with the flat visor, followed by the zero,
oval of looking glass, porthole on a ghost ship,
an opening you stick your arm into and feel nothing.

I want to daydream here in the dark, listening
to the trees behind the house reciting their poems,
bare anonymous beings, murmuring to themselves
in lines that reach out like long branches in spring.
I want my mind to be a sail, susceptible to any breeze
that might be blowing across the lake of consciousness.

But I keep picturing the number, round and daunting:
I drop a fifty-dollar bill on a crowded street,
I carry a fifty-pound bag of wet sand on my shoulders.
I see fifty yearlings leaping a fence in a field,
I fan the five decades before me like a poker hand.

I try contemplating the sufferings of others, Rossini,
for example, considered by many to be the Father
of Modern Insomnia for his prolonged sleeplessness
during the composition of the *William Tell* Overture.

But even a long meditation on the life of Brahms,
widely recognized as the Father of the Modern Lullaby,
will not dispel the fives and zeros, gnomes in the night,
perched on the bedposts, one straddling a closet doorknob.

By dawn, I have become a Catholic again,
the oldest altar boy in the parish, complete
with surplice and cassock, cruet, thurible, and candle.

And this day, whose first light is gilding the windows,
has become another one of the sorrowful mysteries,

following the agony in the garden of childhood
and preceding the crucifixion,
the letter X removed from the word and nailed to a cross,

the rest of the alphabet standing witness
on the rocky hillside, marveling at all the lightning
that is cutting silently across the dark sky.

On Turning Ten

The whole idea of it makes me feel
like I'm coming down with something,
something worse than any stomach ache
or the headaches I get from reading in bad light—
a kind of measles of the spirit,
a mumps of the psyche,
a disfiguring chicken pox of the soul.

You tell me it is too early to be looking back,
but that is because you have forgotten
the perfect simplicity of being one
and the beautiful complexity introduced by two.
But I can lie on my bed and remember every digit.
At four I was an Arabian wizard.
I could make myself invisible
by drinking a glass of milk a certain way.
At seven I was a soldier, at nine a prince.

But now I am mostly at the window
watching the late afternoon light.
Back then it never fell so solemnly
against the side of my tree house,
and my bicycle never leaned against the garage
as it does today,
all the dark blue speed drained out of it.

This is the beginning of sadness, I say to myself,
as I walk through the universe in my sneakers.
It is time to say good-bye to my imaginary friends,
time to turn the first big number.

It seems only yesterday I used to believe
there was nothing under my skin but light.
If you cut me I would shine.
But now when I fall upon the sidewalks of life,
I skin my knees. I bleed.

Shadow

The sun finally goes down like the end
of the Russian novel, and the blinding darkness
over the continent makes me realize

how tired I am of reading and writing,
tired of watching all the dull, horse-drawn sentences
as they plough through fields of paper,

tired of being dragged on a leash of words
by an author I can never look up and see,
tired of examining the exposed spines of books,

I want to be far from the shores of language,
a boat without passengers, lost at sea,
no correspondence, no thesaurus,

not even a name painted across the bow.
Nothing but silence, the kind that falls
whenever I walk outside with a notebook
and a passing cloud darkens my page.

Workshop

I might as well begin by saying how much I like the title.
It gets me right away because I'm in a workshop now
so immediately the poem has my attention,
like the ancient mariner grabbing me by the sleeve.

And I like the first couple of stanzas,
the way they establish this mode of self-pointing
that runs through the whole poem
and tells us that words are food thrown down
on the ground for other words to eat.
I can almost taste the tail of the snake
in its own mouth,
if you know what I mean.

But what I'm not sure about is the voice
which sounds in places very casual, very blue jeans,
but other times seems standoffish,
professorial in the worst sense of the word
like the poem is blowing pipe smoke in my face.
But maybe that's just what it wants to do.

What I did find engaging were the middle stanzas,
especially the fourth one.
I like the image of clouds flying like lozenges
which gives me a very clear picture.
And I really like how this drawbridge operator
just appears out of the blue
with his feet up on the iron railing
and his fishing pole jigging—I like jigging—
a hook in the slow industrial canal below.
I love slow industrial canal below. All those *l*'s.

Maybe it's just me,
but the next stanza is where I start to have a problem.
I mean how can the evening bump into the stars?
And what's an obbligato of snow?
Also, I roam the decaffeinated streets.
At that point I'm lost. I need help.

The other thing that throws me off,
and maybe this is just me,
is the way the scene keeps shifting around.
First, we're in this big aerodrome
and the speaker is inspecting a row of dirigibles,
which makes me think this could be a dream.
Then he takes us into his garden,
the part with the dahlias and the coiling hose,
though that's nice, the coiling hose,
but then I'm not sure where we're supposed to be.
The rain and the mint green light,
that makes it feel outdoors, but what about this wallpaper?
Or is it a kind of indoor cemetery?
There's something about death going on here.

In fact, I start to wonder if what we have here
is really two poems, or three, or four,
or possibly none.

But then there's that last stanza, my favorite.
This is where the poem wins me back,
especially the lines spoken in the voice of the mouse.
I mean we've all seen these images in cartoons before,
but I still love the details he uses
when he's describing where he lives.

The perfect little arch of an entrance in the baseboard,
the bed made out of a curled-back sardine can,
the spool of thread for a table.
I start thinking about how hard the mouse had to work
night after night collecting all these things
while the people in the house were fast asleep,
and that gives me a very strong feeling,
a very powerful sense of something.
But I don't know if anyone else was feeling that.
Maybe that was just me.
Maybe that's just the way I read it.

III

Keats's Handwriting

In print, his poems look as inert as anyone's,
reposing in the open coffin of an anthology,
the type faceless and duplicate,
every letter silent,
the work finished, done for the day.

But here on this thin sheet of manuscript
in the tiny industry of his penmanship
with its loops and flourishes,
leafy stems, broad crosses, and sudden dots,
you can feel the quick jitter of writing,
the animal scratching of the nib,
even the blood beating in the temples.
You can see the light that must have fallen on the page
from an orange candle or a stark winter sun.

Magnified, every minuscule is a photograph;
every indelible accident is a trace of random life,
a moment caught in a spot or fleck,
the thin pen dipped and lifted,
a droplet of ink trembling in the air of the present.

It is enough to make you inhale deeply,
breathe in the brine of the whole century
that held him in her rolling waves
and lapped against the sides of his poems.

And if you lean against the glass case,
bending forward, as he must have over his page,
you can almost see the white linen cuff,
the dark sleeve and the warm, ruddy hand
as if it were your own,

as if your body could fit into his body
the way the life of Shakespeare fits
perfectly into the life of Cervantes.

Then you could rise in the suit of Keats,
walk in his garden, lie on his couch,
the seat of English drowsiness.
And every time you closed your eyes,
you would enter a bower of eglantine
or a liquid glade alive with nymphs.
You would see in the inkwell's black pool
a glossy lake, a musk rose blowing,
night-swollen mushrooms,
and the long, billowing hair of the Muses.

Budapest

My pen moves along the page
like the snout of a strange animal
shaped like a human arm
and dressed in the sleeve of a loose green sweater.

I watch it sniffing the paper ceaselessly,
intent as any forager that has nothing
on its mind but the grubs and insects
that will allow it to live another day.

It wants only to be here tomorrow,
dressed perhaps in the sleeve of a plaid shirt,
nose pressed against the page,
writing a few more dutiful lines

while I gaze out the window and imagine Budapest
or some other city where I have never been.

My Heart

It has a bronze covering inlaid with silver,
originally gilt;
the sides are decorated with openwork zoomorphic
panels depicting events in the history
of an unknown religion.
The convoluted top-piece shows a high
level of relief articulation
as do the interworked spirals at the edges.

It was presumably carried in the house-shaped
reliquary alongside it, an object of exceptional
ornament, one of the few such pieces extant.
The handle, worn smooth, indicates its use
in long-forgotten rituals, perhaps
of a sacrificial nature.

It is engirdled with an inventive example
of gold interlacing, no doubt of Celtic influence.
Previously thought to be a pre-Carolingian work,
it is now considered to be of more recent provenance,
probably the early 1940s.

The ball at the center, visible
through the interstices of the lead webbing
and the elaborate copper grillwork,
is composed possibly of jelly
or an early version of water,
certainly a liquid, remarkably suspended
within the intricate craftsmanship of its encasement.

Romanticism

There are the sick rooms of the nineteenth century
and the faces of the dead in photographs.

There are the symphonic forests of Germany
with dark brooks running through them
and rocks for the distraught to lay their heads.

There is the mantle to lean on,
the grand piano lit with candles,
and a small leather volume of *The Arabian Nights.*

And there is always rain, days and nights of it,
the caretaker asleep in his cottage,
the handle of the wheelbarrow dripping,
the woman in white filling her glass with wine.

And for you, there is the look of the table
you rose from only moments ago,
the way the light from the window seems
to weep on the empty plate, the book of matches,
the thin grape hyacinths in a terra-cotta pot,
as if the sun could feel your absence.

That is the way the light will shine
when you are gone
on all the places your shadow might have fallen:
on a café floor where you could have waited
for someone who was late,
on a lawn where you would have stood
in the green chamber of another summer,

or on a warm run of beach where your shadow
might have reached forever down the sand
in the last glow of daylight
while you surveyed the vastness of the ocean,
hands locked behind your back
in the manner of Vasco Núñez de Balboa.

Monday Morning

The complacency of this student, late
for the final, who chews her pen for an hour,
who sits in her sunny chair,
with a container of coffee and an orange,
a cockatoo swinging freely in her green mind
as if on some drug dissolved,
mingling to give her a wholly ancient rush.
She dreams a little and she fears the mark
she might well get—a catastophe—
as a frown darkens the hauteur of her light brow.
The orange peels and her bright senior ring
make her think of some procession of classmates,
walking across the wide campus, without a sound,
stalled for the passing of her sneakered feet
over the lawn, to silent pals and steins,
dorm of nobody who would bother to pull an A or care.

Dancing Toward Bethlehem

If there is only enough time in the final
minutes of the twentieth century for one last dance
I would like to be dancing it slowly with you,

say, in the ballroom of a seaside hotel.
My palm would press into the small of your back
as the past hundred years collapsed into a pile
of mirrors or buttons or frivolous shoes,

just as the floor of the nineteenth century gave way
and disappeared in a red cloud of brick dust.
There will be no time to order another drink
or worry about what was never said,

not with the orchestra sliding into the sea
and all our attention devoted to humming
whatever it was they were playing.

The First Dream

The wind is ghosting around the house tonight,
and as I lean against the door of sleep
I begin to think about the first person to dream,
how quiet he must have seemed the next morning

as the others stood around the fire
draped in the skins of animals
talking to each other only in vowels,
for this was long before the invention of consonants.

He might have gone off by himself to sit
on a rock and look into the mist of a lake
as he tried to tell himself what had happened,
how he had gone somewhere without going,

how he had put his arms around the neck
of a beast that the others could touch
only after they had killed it with stones,
how he felt its breath on his bare neck.

Then again, the first dream could have come
to a woman, though she would behave,
I suppose, much the same way,
moving off by herself to be alone near water,

except that the curve of her young shoulders
and the tilt of her downcast head
would make her appear to be terribly alone,
and if you were there to notice this,

you might have gone down as the first person
to ever fall in love with the sadness of another.

Sweet Talk

You are not the Mona Lisa
with that relentless look.
Or Venus borne over the froth
of waves on a pink half shell.
Or an odalisque by Delacroix,
veils lapping at your nakedness.

You are more like the sunlight
of Edward Hopper,
especially when it slants
against the eastern side
of a white clapboard house
in the early hours of the morning,
with no figure standing
at a window in a violet bathrobe,
just the sunlight,
the columns of the front porch,
and the long shadows
they throw down
upon the dark green lawn, baby.

Dream

Last night I labored in a cold scriptorium
printing one large block letter at a time,
at work on some crucial document,
a lost epic, the diary of a famous aviator,
a translation from a language I do not know.

Whatever it was, I cannot raise it now
from the deep harbor of sleep
where schools of fish nuzzle the keels of boats,
but I remember writing for hours in pencil
on immense sheets of unlined paper.

Like some Bartleby of the night shift,
my copying was endless,
and as always in dreams, there was someone
who was trying to interfere with me
and someone else, a vague figure

standing off to the side, who wanted to help.
I must ask you which one you were
when I get out of bed and go downstairs
where I can hear you making the tea,
turning the pages of the morning paper.

Man in Space

All you have to do is listen to the way a man
sometimes talks to his wife at a table of people
and notice how intent he is on making his point
even though her lower lip is beginning to quiver,

and you will know why the women in science
fiction movies who inhabit a planet of their own
are not pictured making a salad or reading a magazine
when the men from earth arrive in their rocket,

why they are always standing in a semicircle
with their arms folded, their bare legs set apart,
their breasts protected by hard metal disks.

Philosophy

I used to sit in the café of existentialism,
lost in a blue cloud of cigarette smoke,
contemplating the suicide a tiny Frenchman
might commit by leaping from the rim of my brandy glass.

I used to hunger to be engaged
as I walked the long shaded boulevards,
eyeing women of all nationalities,
a difficult paperback riding in my raincoat pocket.

But these days I like my ontology in an armchair,
a rope hammock, or better still, a warm bath
in a cork-lined room—disengaged, soaking
in the calm, restful waters of speculation.

Afternoons, when I leave the house
for the woods, I think of Aquinas at his desk,
fingers interlocked upon his stomach,
as he deduces another proof for God's existence,

intricate as the branches of these bare November trees.
And as I kick through the leaves and snap
the windfallen twigs, I consider Leibniz on his couch
reaching the astonishing conclusion that monads,

those windowless units of matter, must have souls.
But when I finally reach the top of the hill
and sit down on the flat tonnage of this boulder,
I think of Spinoza, most rarefied of them all.

I look beyond the treetops and the distant ridges
and see him sitting in a beam of Dutch sunlight

slowly stirring his milky tea with a spoon.
Since dawn he has been at his bench grinding lenses,

but now he is leaving behind the saucer and table,
the smoky chimneys and the tile roofs of Amsterdam,
even the earth itself, pale blue, aqueous,
cloud-enshrouded, tilted back on the stick of its axis.

He is rising into that high dome of thought
where loose pages of Shelley float on the air,
where all the formulas of calculus unravel,
tumbling in the radiance of a round Platonic sun—

that zone just below the one where angels accelerate
and the amphitheatrical rose of Dante unfolds.
And now I stand up on the ledge to salute you, Spinoza,
and when I whistle to the dog and start down the hill,

I can feel the thick glass of your eyes upon me
as I step from rock to glacial rock, and on her
as she sniffs her way through the leaves,
her tail straight back, her body low to the ground.

While Eating a Pear

After we have finished here,
the world will continue its quiet turning,
and the years will still transpire,
but now without their numbers,
and the days and months will pass
without the names of Norse and Roman gods.

Time will go by the way it did
before history, pure and unnoticed,
a mystery that arose between the sun and moon
before there was a word
for dawn or noon or midnight,

before there were names for the earth's
uncountable things,
when fruit hung anonymously
from scattered groves of trees,
light on one smooth green side,
shadow on the other.

The End of the World

It is a subject so profound I feel I should
be underwater to think about it properly.
In the most popular version the sky explodes
and horsemen gallop out of the flaming clouds,
pale and bloody, their cloaks flying wickedly.
The disconcerting poetry of Revelations describes
their iron breastplates as being blue as hyacinths.

I have no trouble imagining the oceans boiling away
like forgotten tea water and olive groves turning to ash.
I can even see wheels revolving within wheels,
the mouths of furnaces, and a scarlet beast carrying
the whore of Babylon. I can hear the annunciatory trumpets
and the groans of those who seek death and find it not.

But here in the calm latitudes of this room
I am thinking that the end could be less operatic.
Maybe a black tarpaulin, a kind of boat cover,
could be lowered over the universe one night.
A hand could enter the picture and crumple the cosmos
into a ball of paper and hook it into a waste basket.
A gigantic door might close. A horrible bell could ring.
We could have fire, ice, bang, and whimper all at once.

But who has the time to consider such horrors
when the world's body keeps pressing up against us
with the weight of its beauty, its dizzying sea cliffs
and coasting birds, its rolling fairways and deep pine woods?

Who could imagine all this coming to a sudden end
but the lone visionary we always picture
on a street corner, gaunt, bearded, holding up

the sign that bears the news he cannot keep
to himself: the last headline, the final announcement.

Was it once enough for him to sense the smaller endings?
To know from the way someone combs her hair
one morning that the end of love is near;
to tell by the way the chords make the turn for home
that the end of the song is fast approaching;
or to realize by the tone of afternoon light
that the end of this very day is at hand,
my brethren, and that the summer trees and clouds
will never be blown quite the same way again.

Now it is me down on the floor lettering my sign,
proclaiming that daylight is draining out of the sky.
This is the message I will carry down the gauntlets of the city,
my eyes hollow like those of the dungeoned, the shipwrecked.

Soon it will be evening, and a fuller darkness will descend,
just as I have prophesied, and then, according to my warnings,
we will behold the starry-eyed messiah of the night.

Center

At the first chink of sunrise,
the windows on one side of the house
are frosted with stark orange light,

and in every pale blue window
on the other side
a full moon hangs, a round, white blaze.

I look out one side, then the other,
moving from room to room
as if between countries or parts of my life.

Then I stop and stand in the middle,
extend both arms
like Leonardo's man, naked in a perfect circle.

And when I begin to turn slowly
I can feel the whole house turning with me,
rotating free of the earth.

The sun and moon in all the windows
move, too, with the tips of my fingers,
the solar system turning by degrees

with me, morning's egomaniac,
turning on the hallway carpet in my slippers,
taking the cold orange, blue, and white

for a quiet, unhurried spin,
all wheel and compass, axis and reel,
as wide awake as I will ever be.

Design

I pour a coating of salt on the table
and make a circle in it with my finger.
This is the cycle of life
I say to no one.
This is the wheel of fortune,
the Arctic Circle.
This is the ring of Kerry
and the white rose of Tralee
I say to the ghosts of my family,
the dead fathers,
the aunt who drowned,
my unborn brothers and sisters,
my unborn children.
This is the sun with its glittering spokes
and the bitter moon.
This is the absolute circle of geometry
I say to the crack in the wall,
to the birds who cross the window.
This is the wheel I just invented
to roll through the rest of my life
I say
touching my finger to my tongue.

IV

The Invention of the Saxophone

It was Adolphe Sax, remember,
not Saxo Grammaticus, who gets the ovation.
And by the time he had brought all the components
together—the serpentine shape, the single reed,
the fit of the fingers,
the upward tilt of the golden bell—
it was already 1842, and one gets the feeling
that it was also very late at night.

There is something nocturnal about the sound,
something literally horny,
as some may have noticed on that historic date
when the first odd notes wobbled out of his studio
into the small, darkened town,

summoning the insomniacs (who were up
waiting for the invention of jazz) to their windows,
but leaving the sleepers undisturbed,
even deepening and warming the waters of their dreams.

For this is not the valved instrument of waking,
more the smoky voice of longing and loss,
the porpoise cry of the subconscious.
No one would ever think of blowing reveille
on a tenor without irony.
The men would only lie in their metal bunks,
fingers twined behind their heads,
afloat on pools of memory and desire.

And when the time has come to rouse the dead,
you will not see Gabriel clipping an alto
around his numinous neck.

An angel playing the world's last song
on a glistening saxophone might be enough
to lift them back into the light of earth,
but really no farther.

Once resurrected, they would only lie down
in the long cemetery grass
or lean alone against a lugubrious yew
and let the music do the ascending—
curling snakes charmed from their baskets—
while they wait for the shrill trumpet solo,
that will blow them all to kingdom come.

Medium

The way I like to lay it down sometimes
there is too much traction on paper.
The ink soaks into the cloth of the page.
The words adhere like burrs to a woolen cuff.

I would rather behave on a surface of oil,
a young Renaissance painter in a frock
and a crushed, deep blue velvet hat,
moving the oleaginous colors into the face
of the Virgin or lightening the gray
of the sky behind the oval of her head.

I want to write with the least control,
one finger on the steering wheel,
to write like a watercolorist
whose brush persuades the liquids
to stay above the pull and run of gravity.

I want to hold the pen lightly
as you would touch the stilted, wooden
pointer on a ouija board,
letting it glide over the letters
until it comes to rest as a stone
thrown across a frozen mountain lake
will stop somewhere in the darkness
when the long insistence of friction
has its way and will no longer be overcome.

I would love to write on water
like the final words of Keats
so a current would carry the sentences away

and the slightest breeze would ruffle
the glassy curves of their meaning.

I want to write on air
as in the rapid language of signs
or in the lighting of a cigarette,
both hands cupped near the mouth,
then one waving out the flame
and the long, silent exhalation of smoke,
the gate of the body swinging open.

Most of all,
I want to write on your skin
with the tip of my finger,
printing one capital letter at a time
on the sloping vellum of your back.
I want you to guess the message
being written on your flesh
as children do in summer at the beach,
to feel the shape of every letter
being traced upon your body—oh, ideal reader—
to read with your eyes shut tight,
kneeling in the sand, facing the open sea.

Driving Myself to a Poetry Reading

Halfway there I pull on the headlights
and drift down the road, blazing
like the other cars in the weekday dusk.
I find something on the jazz station
and listen to the chords shifting
under the music like the many gears of the song.
The autumn air is cool and I can see
a few early stars through the windshield,
but like Caesar's Gaul, I feel divided.

There is a part of me that wants
to let go of the wheel, climb over the seat
and fall asleep curled in the back.
This is the part I would like to see
blindfolded some morning, dragged
into a courtyard, and shot.

Another part of me wants to be up on the hood,
a chrome ornament in the shape of a bird
leaning aerodynamically into the wind.
And now I can feel my voice begin to fly
ahead of the car, winging it into the night,
searching the landscape below for a podium,
a shaded lamp, a glass, and a pitcher of water.

This is the part I will still wonder about
when I am dying, staring up at the ceiling,
the part that is eager to perch on the rim
of that glass, wet its hard little beak,
and begin singing every song it ever knew.

Pinup

The murkiness of the local garage is not so dense
that you cannot make out the calendar of pinup
drawings on the wall above a bench of tools.
Your ears are ringing with the sound of
the mechanic hammering on your exhaust pipe,
and as you look closer you notice that this month's
is not the one pushing the lawn mower, wearing
a straw hat and very short blue shorts,
her shirt tied in a knot just below her breasts.
Nor is it the one in the admiral's cap, bending
forward, resting her hands on a wharf piling,
glancing over the tiny anchors on her shoulders.
No, this is March, the month of great winds,
so appropriately it is the one walking her dog
along a city sidewalk on a very blustery day.
One hand is busy keeping her hat down on her head
and the other is grasping the little dog's leash,
so of course there is no hand left to push down
her dress which is billowing up around her waist
exposing her long stockinged legs and yes the secret
apparatus of her garter belt. Needless to say,
in the confusion of wind and excited dog
the leash has wrapped itself around her ankles
several times giving her a rather bridled
and helpless appearance which is added to
by the impossibly high heels she is teetering on.
You would like to come to her rescue,
gather up the little dog in your arms,
untangle the leash, lead her to safety,
and receive her bottomless gratitude, but
the mechanic is calling you over to look

at something under your car. It seems that he has
run into a problem and the job is going
to cost more than he had said and take
much longer than he had thought.
Well, it can't be helped, you hear yourself say
as you return to your place by the workbench,
knowing that as soon as the hammering resumes
you will slowly lift the bottom of the calendar
just enough to reveal a glimpse of what
the future holds in store: ah,
the red polka dot umbrella of April and her
upturned palm extended coyly into the rain.

Piano Lessons

1

My teacher lies on the floor with a bad back
off to the side of the piano.
I sit up straight on the stool.
He begins by telling me that every key
is like a different room
and I am a blind man who must learn
to walk through all twelve of them
without hitting the furniture.
I feel myself reach for the first doorknob.

2

He tells me that every scale has a shape
and I have to learn how to hold
each one in my hands.
At home I practice with my eyes closed.
C is an open book.
D is a vase with two handles.
G flat is a black boot.
E has the legs of a bird.

3

He says the scale is the mother of the chords.
I can see her pacing the bedroom floor
waiting for her children to come home.
They are out at nightclubs shading and lighting
all the songs while couples dance slowly
or stare at one another across tables.
This is the way it must be. After all,

just the right chord can bring you to tears
but no one listens to the scales,
no one listens to their mother.

4

I am doing my scales,
the familiar anthems of childhood.
My fingers climb the ladder of notes
and come back down without turning around.
Anyone walking under this open window
would picture a girl of about ten
sitting at the keyboard with perfect posture,
not me slumped over in my bathrobe, disheveled,
like a white Horace Silver.

5

I am learning to play
"It Might As Well Be Spring"
but my left hand would rather be jingling
the change in the darkness of my pocket
or taking a nap on an armrest.
I have to drag him into the music
like a difficult and neglected child.
This is the revenge of the one who never gets
to hold the pen or wave good-bye,
and now, who never gets to play the melody.

6

Even when I am not playing, I think about the piano.
It is the largest, heaviest,

and most beautiful object in this house.
I pause in the doorway just to take it all in.
And late at night I picture it downstairs,
this hallucination standing on three legs,
this curious beast with its enormous moonlit smile.

Exploring the Coast of Birdland

This time it wasn't a sea gull landing on a spar
or the offshore aroma of wild flowers
but the faint sound of a drum solo
that told us we were nearing land.
By midnight we had rounded the treacherous
point called Cape Monk on the charts
and were headed down the windward coast
past the twinkling lights of Goofport,
making safe passage through the choppy waters
by keeping the tune always to starboard
and the open sea to port.
All night we lay out on the broad deck
watching the stars in the rigging
and listening to the cool, driving music
as it slid across the phosphorous sea
and washed over our barely moving ship.

We followed the contours of the island,
and by the first feathery lights of dawn
we entered the Bay of Riffs
and lined up along the taffrail
to observe the natives on the shoreline,
many jamming under the tall palms,
others walking along the crescent beach,
heads lowered in concentration,
instruments cradled,
and a few standing in the small, ankle-splashing
waves as the sun rose slowly into their faces.

I remember the sweet, nutty smoke
that drifted from their smoldering fires
and the heavy tenor solo that someone was pouring

over the chords to "All the Things You Are"
as we dropped anchor
and the crew made ready to row ashore.
I remember looking into my tilted shaving mirror
and seeing the reflection of the pink sky
as if in the window of the morning.
Then I wet my razor and drew it,
shining, along the borders of my dark goatee.

The Blues

Much of what is said here
must be said twice,
a reminder that no one
takes an immediate interest in the pain of others.

Nobody will listen, it would seem,
if you simply admit
your baby left you early this morning
she didn't even stop to say good-bye.

But if you sing it again
with the help of the band
which will now lift you to a higher,
more ardent and beseeching key,

people will not only listen;
they will shift to the sympathetic
edges of their chairs,
moved to such acute anticipation

by that chord and the delay that follows,
they will not be able to sleep
unless you release with one finger
a scream from the throat of your guitar

and turn your head back to the microphone
to let them know
you're a hard-hearted man
but that woman's sure going to make you cry.

Nightclub

You are so beautiful and I am a fool
to be in love with you
is a theme that keeps coming up
in songs and poems.
There seems to be no room for variation.
I have never heard anyone sing
I am so beautiful
and you are a fool to be in love with me,
even though this notion has surely
crossed the minds of women and men alike.
You are so beautiful, too bad you are a fool
is another one you don't hear.
Or, you are a fool to consider me beautiful.
That one you will never hear, guaranteed.

For no particular reason this afternoon
I am listening to Johnny Hartman
whose dark voice can curl around
the concepts of love, beauty, and foolishness
like no one else's can.
It feels like smoke curling up from a cigarette
someone left burning on a baby grand piano
around three o'clock in the morning;
smoke that billows up into the bright lights
while out there in the darkness
some of the beautiful fools have gathered
around little tables to listen,
some with their eyes closed,
others leaning forward into the music
as if it were holding them up,
or twirling the loose ice in a glass,
slipping by degrees into a rhythmic dream.

Yes, there is all this foolish beauty,
borne beyond midnight,
that has no desire to go home,
especially now when everyone in the room
is watching the large man with the tenor sax
that hangs from his neck like a golden fish.
He moves forward to the edge of the stage
and hands the instrument down to me
and nods that I should play.
So I put the mouthpiece to my lips
and blow into it with all my living breath.
We are all so foolish,
my long bebop solo begins by saying,
so damn foolish
we have become beautiful without even knowing it.

Some Final Words

I cannot leave you without saying this:
the past is nothing,
a nonmemory, a phantom,
a soundproof closet in which Johann Strauss
is composing another waltz no one can hear.

It is a fabrication, best forgotten,
a wellspring of sorrow
that waters a field of bitter vegetation.

Leave it behind.
Take your head out of your hands
and arise from the couch of melancholy
where the window-light falls against your face
and the sun rides across the autumn sky,
steely behind the bare trees,
glorious as the high strains of violins.

But forget Strauss.
And forget his younger brother,
the poor bastard who was killed in a fall
from a podium while conducting a symphony.

Forget the past,
forget the stunned audience on its feet,
the absurdity of their formal clothes
in the face of sudden death,
forget their collective gasp,
the murmur and huddle over the body,
the creaking of the lowered curtain.

Forget Strauss
with that encore look in his eye

and his tiresome industry:
more than five hundred finished compositions!
He even wrote a polka for his mother.
That alone is enough to make me flee the past,
evacuate its temples,
and walk alone under the stars
down these dark paths strewn with acorns,
feeling nothing but the crisp October air,
the swing of my arms
and the rhythm of my stepping—
a man of the present who has forgotten
every composer, every great battle,
just me,
a thin reed blowing in the night.

BILLY COLLINS

        is professor of English at Lehman College
of the City University of New York. His poems have been
published in *The New Yorker, The Paris Review, Poetry,
American Poetry Review, The American Scholar, Harper's,*
and many other magazines, and he is the recipient of
fellowships from the National Endowment for the Arts
and the Guggenheim Foundation, among others. *Questions
About Angels* was a winner of the National Poetry Series
publication prize. *The Art of Drowning* is his fifth book of
poetry. He lives in Somers, New York.

PITT POETRY SERIES

Ed Ochester, General Editor